Why Is This Day Special?
Harvest Festival

Jillian Powell

A⁺
Smart Apple Media

First published in 2005 by Franklin Watts
96 Leonard Street, London EC2A 4XD

Franklin Watts Australia
45–51 Huntley Street, Alexandria, NSW 2015

Series editor: Sarah Peutrill, Art director: Jonathan Hair, Designer: Ian Thompson, Picture researcher: Diana Morris, Reading consultant: Margaret Perkins, Institute of Education, University of Reading

Picture credits: Mike Alkins/Eye Ubiquitous: 7t. Tom Allwood/Alamy: 14. David Cummings/Eye Ubiquitous: 13b. Dinodia: 15t, 25, 29. I. Genut/Art Directors/Trip: 11b. F. Good/Art Directors/Trip: 13t. HAGA/AI Pix: 22bl. Juliet Highet/Hutchison: 27. Ibrahim/Art Directors/Trip: 9b. Image Works/Topham: cover main image, 9t. Andres Krusberg/Wirepix/Image Works/Topham: 22tr. James H. Pickerell/Image Works/Topham: 6, 18. Picturepoint/Topham: 10, 15b, 17t. Jackie & Allan Reditt/Hutchison: 23. Resource Foto/Art Directors/Trip: 3, 21bl. Helene Rogers/Art Directors/Trip: 7b, 19t, 26bl. Brian Seed/Art Directors/Trip: 16b, 24t. Paul Seheult/Eye Ubiquitous: 12b. S Shapiro/Art Directors/Trip: 8, 11t. Topham: cover br, 24b. P. Treanor/Art Directors/Trip: 19b. Charles Walker/Topham: 20b.

Published in the United States by Smart Apple Media
2140 Howard Drive West, North Mankato, Minnesota 56003

U.S. publication copyright © 2007 Smart Apple Media

Library of Congress Cataloging-in-Publication Data

Powell, Jillian.
Harvest festival / by Jillian Powell.
p. cm. — (Why is this day special?)
Includes index.
ISBN-13 : 978-1-58340-950-3
1. Harvest festivals—Juvenile literature. I. Title.

GT4380.P68 2006
394.264—dc22   2005052550

9 8 7 6 5 4 3 2 1

Contents

Harvest festivals

People have celebrated harvest festivals for thousands of years.

Wheat is one of the world's main harvests. This crop is being harvested in North America.

Harvest is the time when crops are picked. If the crop is good, people celebrate because there is plenty to eat. In some parts of the world, a bad harvest may mean that people go hungry.

In northern lands, such as Europe, most crops are harvested from August to October. In southern lands, such as Australia, they are harvested from December to March.

" At school we learned about harvest festivals and found out about the food that people eat all over the world. "

Simone, age 9

In countries where there are wet and dry seasons, crops are harvested in the dry season. In some places, crops are harvested all year.

All around the world, people have found ways to celebrate a good harvest.

Carnival dancers celebrate the "crop over" festival in Barbados.

These children are printing fall leaves for a harvest wall display.

Giving thanks

Harvest is a time for giving thanks.

Christians celebrate harvest festivals in churches and schools. They sing hymns and say prayers of thanks to God for the harvest.

Many people give thanks with the "first fruits." These are the first harvested foods of the season. They might be fruit, vegetables, or cereals. Jewish people celebrate a festival called Shavuot in May or June each year. They decorate their homes and offer the first fruits of the harvest to God.

Jewish children take part in a first fruits ceremony for Shavuot.

Black African people around the world celebrate Kwanzaa—the first fruits of harvest—for seven days in December and January. It is a time for giving thanks and remembering ancestors.

This boy is lighting a candle in a *kinara*, a candleholder used at Kwanzaa.

> " *At Kwanzaa, we light seven candles, one for each day of the festival. They stand on a straw mat, with an ear of corn for each child in the family.* "
>
> Gus, age 9

In many parts of Africa and Asia, it is also tradition to offer the first fruits of harvest to the gods in December.

During the Mehregan Festival harvest celebrations in Iran, dates and other fruits are gathered.

Remembering

Some harvest festivals remind people of times from the past.

At Thanksgiving, Americans remember the first good harvest of the Pilgrims in 1621. The Pilgrims were the first English people who went to live in America. When they arrived, the Native Americans helped them, and their harvest was good. They celebrated for three days.

> " *I really look forward to Thanksgiving, because everyone in the family gets together to celebrate.* "
> *Theresa, age 9*

Today, families celebrate Thanksgiving every year on the fourth Thursday in November. They give thanks for the blessings of the past year.

The Pilgrims celebrate their first Thanksgiving.

Jewish people celebrate the festival of Sukkot in September or October. They remember the time when farmers lived in shelters by the fields to help them quickly gather in the harvest.

At Sukkot, Jews also remember the time when their ancestors were living in shelters in the desert, before they found a home in Israel.

Many Jews build their own shelter at Sukkot. It has three sides and is called a Sukkah. They may hang fruit and flowers from it and eat their meals inside it.

Most synagogues and temples build a public Sukkah where Jews can celebrate Sukkot together.

Celebrating plenty

Harvest is a time for celebrating plenty.

Christian harvest festivals celebrate crops such as wheat and oats. This is because these crops are an important part of the diet in many countries where Christians live.

Wheat is an important crop because it is used to make bread.

In Asia, many festivals celebrate the rice harvest.

Rice is an important food in Asia.

In Japan, people feast, dance, and drink rice wine after the harvest in August.

These children are carrying a tray of rice wine, called *sake*.

Rice is also important in India. The Hindu harvest festival of Pongal lasts for three days in January. Rice plays an important part in the celebrations.

This is part of the Pongal celebrations. At this time, Hindus cook a sweet rice pudding, which they offer to the gods of the sun and the rain.

Women decorate their doorsteps with colorful patterns of rice flour at Pongal.

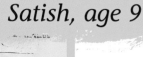

At Pongal, Mom boils milky rice pudding in a new pot and lets it boil over, then we shout, 'Pongal, Pongal!'

Satish, age 9

Animal harvests

Some harvest festivals celebrate the importance of animals such as sheep and cattle.

The second day of the Hindu festival of Pongal in India celebrates cattle. People offer prayers for cows, bulls, and other farm animals.

Each family chooses a cow to decorate with flowers, beads, colorful cloth, and powders.

They feed the cow with boiled rice and then walk it in a procession.

" Mathu Pongal is the day when we celebrate the animals. It's exciting watching the races with bulls. "

Satish, age 9

At Pongal, there are also games and contests as young men race bulls and try to snatch money that is tied to them.

At Pongal, children dress up as animals for fun.

Two boys dress up as a snake and a zebra at the Pongal festival.

In Australia, sheep farmers celebrate the harvest of wool. They hold sheep-shearing festivals in November, when the sheep's winter wool is shorn, or shaved off.

These men are taking part in a sheep-shearing contest on an Australian farm.

Harvest of the seas

Fish are the harvest of the seas, and this harvest is also celebrated.

In many places where fish are important, there is a ceremony every year to bless the fishing boats and celebrate the fish harvest. Christian churches are decorated for the harvest festival with fishing nets and equipment.

At the church of Saint Mary-at-Hill, near the Billingsgate fish market in London, England, there is a harvest festival on the first Sunday in October, at the end of the fishing season.

Fishermen at Argungu take part in a contest to catch the most fish.

In Argungu, Nigeria, a fishing festival is held for three days in February each year on the Sokoto River. It celebrates the start of the fishing season.

People are allowed to catch as many fish as they can. There are prizes for the best fishermen and the fastest swimmers.

" At our fishing festival, you can watch canoe and swimming races. "
Jamilah, age 8

Harvest meals

Feasts and family meals are an important part of many harvest celebrations.

Thanksgiving day in America is a public holiday. Families and friends get together for a big meal of roast turkey with cranberry sauce and pumpkin pie.

Many American families say a prayer of thanks before enjoying their feast.

In China, the Moon Festival celebrates the rice harvest at the time of the full moon in August. Families hang lanterns from houses and trees, and have a feast or picnic with moon cakes.

Moon cakes are round cakes with sweet fillings made from beans or seeds. Some have egg yolks inside that look like a bright full moon.

Children are allowed to stay up late to watch the full moon rise.

These children are lighting candles for their Moon Festival picnic.

" At the Moon Festival, children can make a wish to the Lady of the Moon to make their dreams come true. "

Lien, age 8

Harvest customs

There are many different harvest customs around the world.

Corn dolls are made from the last straw of the harvest. People once believed a corn goddess lived in the crops. At the end of the harvest, they made the last bundle of straw into a corn doll to keep the goddess safe.

When the field was plowed, the corn doll was buried or burned, so the goddess would go back into the land and give a good harvest the next year.

Corn dolls are made in different shapes, such as a doll, fan, moon, or spiral.

" Someone came into our class to show us how corn dolls were made. Then we made some dolls with dried flowers and wheat. "

Sasha, age 9

Special loaves of bread are baked in the shape of a sheaf of wheat for harvest displays. They remind people that bread comes from the harvest of wheat.

A loaf of bread baked for a harvest display.

Flowers are important at the harvest festival of Onam in August and September, in southern India. Homes are decorated with flower garlands, and flower petals are spread in patterns on the grass.

This girl is carrying a tray of flower petals for Onam.

Harvest parades

In many parts of the world, people celebrate the harvest with parades.

At Thanksgiving in America, there is a huge parade in New York. Giant balloons are carried through the streets, and school bands march and play music.

Giant balloons are popular at the Thanksgiving parade in New York.

In Japan, crowds gather to watch the Lantern Festival, which celebrates the rice harvest in August. Young men parade through the streets, balancing bamboo poles that carry hundreds of paper lanterns.

At the Lantern Festival, each paper lantern stands for a grain of rice.

In Tomar in Portugal, there is a harvest festival called the Festival of the Trays every four years in July. Girls parade through the streets with trays on their heads carrying fruit and flowers.

" My sister carried a tray at this year's harvest festival. She said it was very heavy, but I want to carry one when I'm older. "

Melissa, age 8

At the festival in Tomar, each girl carries a tray holding 30 bread rolls decorated with wheat and paper flowers.

Harvest fun

Harvest is a happy time, celebrated with games and sports, music and dancing.

At the Yam Festival in Ghana in August, the Ashanti people celebrate with drumming and dancing.

In southern India, there are river races of long boats to celebrate Pongal and Onam.

Dancers in Ghana celebrate the yam, a vegetable that grows in hot countries (shown below).

Thousands of people gather to cheer on the boats at the Onam festival in India.

Singing and dancing are part of many celebrations, such as the Japanese Lantern Festival for the rice harvest in August and the Sikh festival of Baisakhi in April.

Baisakhi is a celebration to thank God for a good harvest for the year and also the coming year. Sikhs wear their best clothes and dance to show their joy.

> *" Baisakhi is an important time because it's the start of the Sikh New Year as well as a harvest festival. "*
>
> Sunita, age 9

Sikhs perform a dance during Baisakhi that describes the acts of sowing and harvesting crops.

Giving and sharing

Harvest is a time for sharing food.

At Christian harvest festivals in schools and churches, people bring gifts of food. They may bring fruit and vegetables that they have grown, or cans and boxes of food that they have bought. The food is given to the homeless and those in need.

A child delivers a harvest gift to an elderly person.

66 *After our harvest assembly, we made boxes with gifts of food, and we took them to old people who live near our school.* 99

Matthew, age 9

Food is blessed before it is given to the poor in Thailand.

In Buddhist countries, such as Thailand, people take harvest gifts of food to temples to be blessed before they are shared among the poor.

There are millions of people in the world who do not have enough to eat. In some countries, if the harvest is bad, many people go hungry and die.

Harvest is a time to give thanks that we have enough food to eat, and to share our food with others.

Glossary

ancestors the people in our families who lived long before us.

blessings words said to bring goodness or happiness.

corn doll a doll or other shape made from straw after a crop harvest.

custom an act that is repeated over many years.

first fruits the first crops or fruits from a harvest.

goddess a female god.

hymn a song of praise or thanks to God.

Native Americans the people who lived in North America and Canada before others came to live there.

Pilgrims the first English people to settle in North America in 1620.

plowed when the soil in a field is turned over and made ready for sowing seed.

prayer words spoken to God.

procession a gathering of people, floats, or vehicles moving along together.

sheaf a bundle tied together.

shearing cutting wool from an animal.

synagogue a building where Jewish people go to pray and study.

tradition a belief or custom that has been passed from one generation to another.

Religions in this book

Buddhism
Follower: Buddhist
Important figure: Siddhartha Gautama, the Buddha
Gods: none—the Buddha did not want people to worship him as a God
Place of worship: Viharas (temples or monasteries), stupas (shrines)
Holy books: Tirpitaka (Pali Canon), Diamond Sutra, and others

Christianity
Follower: Christian
Important figure: Jesus Christ, Son of God
God: One God as Father, Son, and Holy Spirit
Places of worship: Churches, cathedrals, and chapels
Holy books: the Bible

Hinduism
Follower: Hindu
Gods: Many gods and goddesses, including Brahma (the Creator), Vishnu (the Protector), and Shiva (the Destroyer)
Places of worship: Mandirs (temples) and shrines
Holy books: Vedas, Upanishads, Ramayana, Mahabharata

Judaism
Follower: Jew
Important figures: Abraham, Isaac, Jacob, and Moses
God: One God, the creator
Place of worship: Synagogue
Holy Books: Tenakh, Torah, Talmud

Sikhism
Follower: Sikh
Important figure: Guru Nanak
God: One God
Place of worship: Gurdwaras (temples)
Holy book: Guru Granth Sahib

Index